CHINESE PROVERBS

中國成語

Illustrated by You Shan Tang

COLLECTED BY RUTHANNE LUM McCUNN

Chronicle Books • San Francisco

Printed in Hong Kong.

ISBN: 0-8118-0083-0

Library of Congress Cataloging in Publication Data
available.

Book and cover design by Myrna Chiu/
Woman with a Knife Graphics
Chinese typography by Katherine Loh Graphic Design, Inc.
Cover illustration by You Shan Tang

Distributed in Canada by Raincoast Books,
112 East Third Avenue, Vancouver, B.C. V5T 1C8

10 9 8 7 6 5 4 3 2 1

Chronicle Books
275 Fifth Street
San Francisco, CA 94103

眼闊肚窄

The eyes are wide but the stomach is narrow.

狡兔三窟

The cunning hare has three burrows.

下雨擋風才是好朋友。

A good friend shields you from the storm.

人怕出名豬怕壯。

As a pig fears getting fat, so a man
fears renown.

虎鹿不同行。

Tigers and deer do not walk together.

螞蟻能搬山。

Ants can move even a mighty mountain.

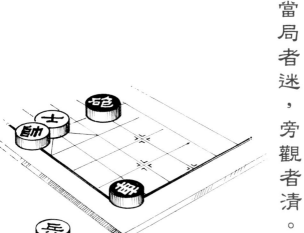

當局者迷，旁觀者清。

Observers can see a chess game more
clearly than the players.

真金不怕火煉。

Genuine gold fears no fire.

天下烏鴉一般黑。

Crows are black the world over.

星星之火，可以燎原。

A single spark can set a prairie on fire.

狡兔死，走狗烹。

When the rabbits are dead, the hounds
that tracked them will be cooked.

11

畫餅充飢

You cannot satisfy hunger by
drawing a cake.

伴君如伴虎。

Serving the powerful is like sleeping
with a tiger.

江山易改，本性難移。

Rivers and mountains are more
easily changed than a man's nature.

路遙知馬力，日久見人心。

Distance tests the endurance of a horse; time reveals a man's character.

樹倒猢猻散。

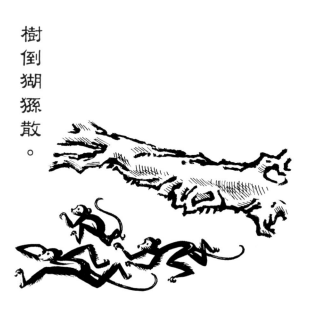

When a tree falls, the monkeys scatter.

水能載舟，也能覆舟。

Water can both sustain and sink a ship.

騎
虎
難
下

It is difficult to get off a tiger's back.

燕雀豈知鴻鵠之志。

A swallow cannot know
the lofty ambitions of an eagle.

19

不入虎穴，焉得虎子。

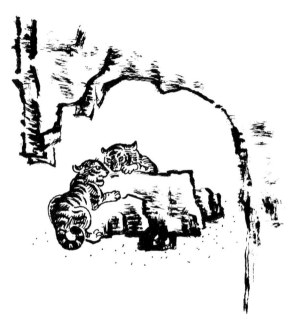

If you do not brave the tiger's lair,
how can you capture the cub?

20

飲水思源

When you drink water,
remember the source.

21

狗瘦主人羞。

A lean dog shames its master.

水滴石穿

Water can drip through stone.

聚蚊成雷

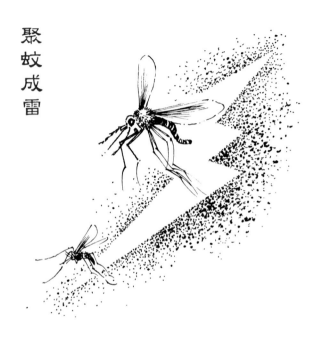

A swarm of mosquitoes can sound
like thunder.

天下無不散之筵席。

On earth no feast lasts forever.

明槍易躲，暗箭難防。

It is easy to dodge a spear you can see, difficult to guard against an arrow shot from hiding.

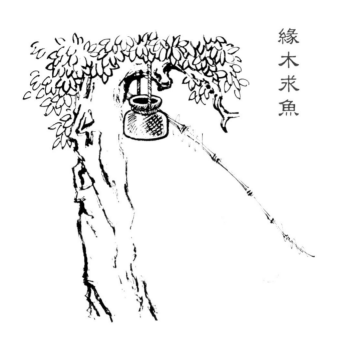

緣木求魚

Do not climb a tree to look for fish.

臨淵羨魚，不如退而結網。

Better to make a net than to yearn for
fish at the edge of a pond.

種瓜得瓜，種豆得豆。

Sow melon, reap melon; sow beans,
reap beans.

好蜂不採落地花。

A good bee never takes pollen from a fallen flower.

窮鼠齧貓

A cornered rat will bite the cat.

人無笑臉不開店。

A person without a smiling face should
not open a shop.

殺雞焉用牛刀。

You do not need a butcher's knife to kill a chicken.

木本水源

A tree has its roots, a stream its source.

狗嘴裡吐不出象牙。

Ivory does not come out of
a dog's mouth.

老馬識途

An old horse knows the way.

良
藥
苦
口

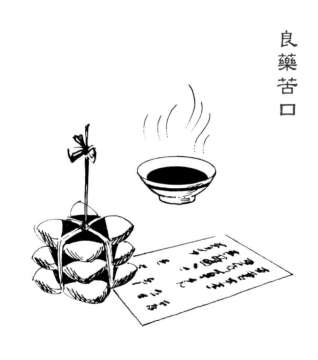

Good medicine is bitter to the taste.

拔苗助長

You cannot help shoots grow by
pulling them up.

寧爲雞口，勿爲牛後。

Better to be a rooster's beak than
a bull's rump.

樹欲靜而風不止。

Trees may prefer calm, but the wind
will not subside.

40

鼠目寸光

A mouse can see only an inch.

臨渴掘井

Do not wait until you're thirsty to dig a well.

42

麻雀雖小，五臟俱全。

The sparrow may be small but it has
all the vital organs.

斬
草
除
根

When weeding, destroy the roots.

殺雞取卵

Do not kill the hen for her eggs.

馬死落地行。

If the horse dies, then you have to walk.

鼠有鼠道

Rats know the way of rats.

孤
掌
難
鳴

You cannot clap with one hand.

48

各花入各眼。

Flowers look different to different eyes.

人靠衣裳馬靠鞍。

A man is judged by his clothes,
a horse by its saddle.

50

覆水難收

Spilt water cannot be retrieved.

一腳不踏二船。

One foot cannot stand on two boats.

盡信書不如無書。

Better to do without books than to
believe everything they say.

不上高山，不顯平地。

If you do not climb the mountain,
you will not see the plain.

人心不足蛇吞象。

An avaricious person is like a snake
trying to swallow an elephant.

畫龍點睛

When you paint a dragon, dot its eyes.

不管黑貓白貓，抓到老鼠就是好貓。

It does not matter if the cat is
black or white so long as it catches rats.

57

佛口蛇心

Beware the person with a Buddha's mouth and a snake's heart.